Foreword

Congratulations to Ariane Durden! It is exciting to witness the future of health as it continues to expand with new vision and excitement for our children. Featuring superkids as "Superheroes eat the rainbow!" offers ways to capture the imagination of children in ways that leave a lifelong impact on the way they approach making healthy nutritional choices.

As past Chairman to the President's Council on Sports and Fitness, I highly recommend this amazing book for parents, teachers, and especially children.

Yours in Health,

Lee Haney
Chairman to the President's Council on Sports and Fitness
8 times Mr. Olympia
Founder of The International Association of Fitness and Science

Note to Parents

This book encourages your children to eat healthy foods and exercise through play. Healthy food choices and activity help fight childhood obesity. Super Sasha Jones serves as a role model to encourage them to make healthy choices. Tell your children to recite "A Superhero's Creed," and do what it says. They will become "Superheroes!"

Dedication

Inspired by First Lady Michelle Obama's *Let's Move!* Initiative

This book is dedicated to raising a healthier generation of kids by encouraging them to eat healthily and make healthy lifestyle choices to solve the problem of childhood obesity. Thank you Mom, Dad, G. Michael, Dr. Cotwright, Mr. Haney, and all of the superheroes in my life who helped me make this book possible.

Love,

C. Ariane Durden

Becoming a Superhero

By C. Ariane Durden

Featuring Super Sasha Jones

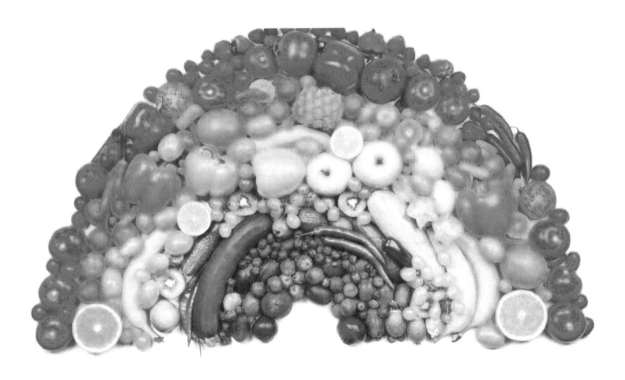

"Superheroes eat the rainbow!"™

Kaboom! Kaboom! Kaboom! Do you want to learn how to become a superhero? Ready! Set! Go! Imagine being as strong as a panther and splashing through sparkling water! Imagine running faster than lightning!

Today is race day in Peach City for one kid to learn how to become a superhero! The first kid to find the secret recipe wins. Surprisingly, the secret recipe goes missing! Sasha Jones and Eva Smith race to be first to find the secret recipe. Help them find the secret recipe, and learn how to become a superhero.

At home, Sasha asks her parents, "What makes superheroes super?"

Mama says, "Eat superfoods the colors of the rainbow. Red, orange, yellow, green, blue, and purple. Eat the rainbow!"

Daddy says, "Exercise by playing outside and move to build strong muscles."

Sasha eats a super breakfast. She eats

SuperherO's cereal with strawberries and milk. She has

a huge boiled egg and a delicious red apple. The apple is

sweet and good for her heart. She drinks milk to make

her bones strong. Eva eats cheese pizza and a

chocolate chip cookie. She drinks soda for breakfast.

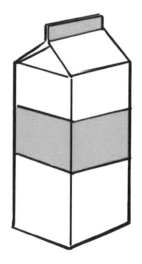

At school, Sasha asks Coach Mike, "What makes superheroes super?" "Using all three superpowers like super brain power, super energy, and super strength," he answers. Sasha memorizes what he says.

At lunch, Sasha asks her friends what makes superheroes super. Yasmine says, "Super energy!" Brandon says, "Super strong bones!" Paris says, "Having both super energy and super strong bones." Sasha says, "Hmmm! Maybe superfoods help superheroes get super powers. The more superfoods you eat, the more superpowers you get." Eva laughs and tells her, "You can't become a superhero by eating superfoods."

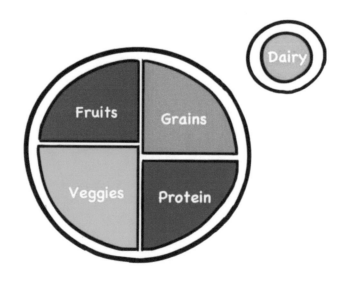

Sasha and Eva line up at the starting line. Coach Mike tells them to follow the rainbow from Gooey Apple Mountain to Grapevine Palace.

He says, "You may find surprises along the way. Eat the rainbow, and get superpowers. Whoever finds the recipe first and does what it says, becomes a superhero."

Coach Mike yells, "Get ready, set, go!"

Sasha and Eva speed towards Gooey Apple Mountain like a rollercoaster. Sasha believes the superhero recipe is at the top of the mountain. Eva grabs Sasha's shoe laces. Sasha starts to fall on her face. Eva laughs and zooms up the mountain. She gets there first and finds a yummy, chocolate fudge sundae with sprinkles.

Gooey Apple Mountain has delicious red apples and gooey peanut butter. Peanut butter has protein which builds and makes strong muscles. Sasha refuels with a delicious apple and yummy peanut butter. She drinks lots of water.

Zip! Zap! Zoom! Sasha speeds toward Optic-man Omari and Dreamsicle Museum with her magic zip-line rope. It has oranges, carrots, and peaches splashing in orange drops.

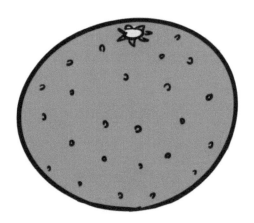

Optic-man Omari tells Sasha to eat carrots to get super vision. This helps her to see the orange slime trap. She uses her super vision to see Eva riding a bus to Enchanting Evergreen Jungle. Eva thinks she will never catch up.

smarta

Sasha sprints to Blazing Banana Park. Blazing Yasmine tells Sasha to eat bananas for super energy. Bananas help her run super fast and get super brain power. She takes a break and enjoys a banana smoothie.

She knows she is almost there to Grapevine Palace.

Zip! Zap! Zoom! With a burst of energy, Sasha speeds towards Enchanting Evergreen Jungle. It has dark green leafy vegetables like spinach, kale, collards, and cabbage for strong bones. Hiding in the jungle are delicious pickles, green beans, green peas, and broccoli.

Eva is surprised to see Sasha has caught up to her. Sasha zooms past Eva, making her seem as slow as a turtle. She leaves Eva in a pile of dust.

Sasha uses her super energy and super vision to avoid the

traps, but it is too late. Eva made a sticky bubblegum

trap to slow her down. Like magic, Eva uses super jet

skates to zip past her. Sasha is ready to quit,

but she does not give up!

Sasha used her super energy to break loose. She

meets Brave Heart Brandon at Blueberry Aquarium.

He tells her to eat blueberries for a strong heart.

She pops three blueberries into her mouth.

BLUEBERRY AQUARIUM

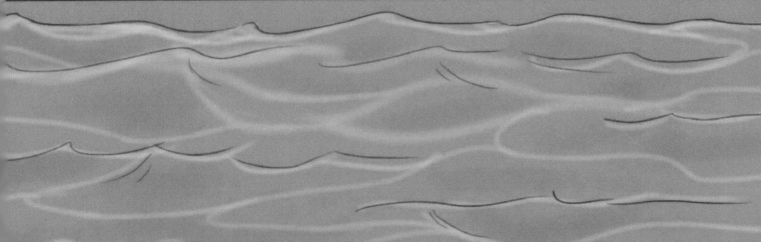

Splash! Splash!! Splash!!! The blueberries give her energy to swim very fast. She swims through the water to Grapevine Palace. There she meets Super Paris who gives her four grapes. She eats them to get more energy.

Sasha remembers to use super brain power, super energy, and super strength. She climbs to the top of Grapevine Palace as fast as she can. Eva struggles to climb to the top.

Eva cheats and uses her last bit of jet fuel to blast up

to the finish line. She finds the superhero recipe, but

it is blank! Eva is confused. She says,

"What's going on here?"

Coach Mike lands at the finish line and declares

Sasha the winner. He explains that

Sasha is first to find the recipe.

Coach Mike says, "The true recipe was hidden

throughout the race in the healthy choices she made!"

Kaboom! Kaboom!! Kaboom!!! Fireworks go off!

Sasha is rewarded with her own super suit. She

becomes Super Sasha Jones! She gets inducted into

the Superhero Hall of Fame which includes her family

and friends. You can find Super Sasha Jones eating

healthily and playing outside around Peach City.

Super Sasha Jones knows that you can become a superhero too! Eat healthy foods, exercise, and drink lots of milk and water. "Recite A Superhero's Creed," and do what it says. Super heroes are everywhere!

A Superhero's Creed

- A superhero eats the rainbow.

- A superhero drinks lots of milk and water.

- A superhero exercises and gets moving.

- A superhero does good and helps others.

- A superhero never gives up.

I am a superhero!

About the Author: C. Ariane Durden is a nutrition educator and author who has spent the last decade advocating good nutrition and exercises as means to fight childhood obesity. Her debut fantasy book is *Becoming a Superhero*, which uses southern charm and a cast of multicultural characters to encourage children to eat superfoods and become "superheroes." *Becoming a Superhero* is dedicated to raising a healthier generation of kids by encouraging them to eat healthily and make healthy lifestyle choices to solve the problem of childhood obesity.

Ariane was inspired by First Lady Michelle Obama's **Let's Move!** Initiative while studying nutrition in Dr. Cotwright's class at the University of Georgia in 2014. She earned her B.S. degree in Family and Consumer Sciences in 2015. Since that time, she began to look for ways to motivate kids to eat healthily and exercise in fun and different ways. She thought of a way to use the food rainbow to encourage kids to eat superfoods to gain superpowers and a storyline to encourage activity. Thus, Becoming a Superhero was born in 2019. The copyright, edits, and illustrations were completed in 2020. Topped by food rainbows, her two trademarks--Superheroes eat the rainbow! and Superkids eat the rainbow! are being registered.

Ariane is a member of the Society of Children's Book Writers and Illustrators, Southern Breeze Branch. She loves staying active, whether that's traveling on a cruise or exercising near her home in College Park, renamed South Fulton, Georgia. She is dedicated to improving children's nutrition one plate at a time.

You can follow the adventures of Super Sasha Jones
at www.supersashajones.com
& Instagram @supersashajones.

About the Illustrator: DeVonn Armstrong is a graphic designer and illustrator who lives in Decatur, Georgia. He was born in Atlanta and raised in Jackson, Mississippi. He graduated from Mississippi State University with a degree in Fine Arts. DeVonn specializes in comics, graphic novels, and children's books and enjoys inspiring others through good storytelling and visual art. He has a particular passion for stories involving fantasy, science fiction, and of course...superheroes. When he's not illustrating, DeVonn enjoys learning something new through a podcast, relaxing with a video game, or traveling with his wife Lataisha.

You can find more of his work on devonnarmstrong.com
& on Instagram @isaiah_theillustrated.

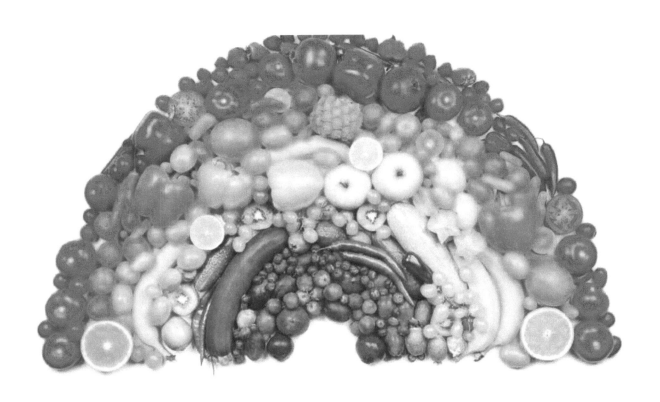

"Superkids eat the rainbow!"™

AMAZON 5-STAR REVIEWS

"This beautiful little book has a noble aim of encouraging healthy behaviors."
Ronald B. Foster--

"This is an excellent book that will help teach and motivate children to make healthy choices." Beverly Thomas

"The book kept my grandson entertained throughout the entire book."
V. Sanford

"Easy reading for children! "Good teaching illustrations!"
B. Mays

"A very nice read about nutrition for the youths of today and a refresher to older people about the basic food group for better nutrition as we age."
J. Mitchell

"...Our kids are suffering from obesity and chronic illnesses, eating high fat and empty caloric foods. Seeing Superhero Sasha letting kids know, they can be strong and healthy by eating fruits and vegetables, this makes them heroes. Amazing format." R. Clark, RN

"As a Microbiologist, I really found "Becoming a Superhero" so helpful, because it describes how each vegetable helps our body to function ." ...
T. Sacro

"... As a healthcare professional, I plan to use this in my practice."
S. Hopewell

"... a great tool to use when working with my kiddos in therapy session."
J. Dawson OTR/L

"A timely book to help the next generation look beyond where they are for inspiration!"
J. Latimer

"This generation of kids will be so thrilled to read this and carry out the healthy choices that they have learned through this book!"
Dr. Chinnaya Ukpabi

Printed in the USA
CPSIA information can be obtained
at www.ICGtesting.com
LVHW072157121124
796203LV00058B/35